EASY PIANO

Disney

FROZEN II

MUSIC FROM THE MOTION PICTURE SOUNDTRACK

ISBN 978-1-5400-8310-4

Hal•Leonard®

Visit Hal Leonard Online at
www.halleonard.com

Contact us:
Hal Leonard
7777 West Bluemound Road
Milwaukee, WI 53213
Email: info@halleonard.com

In Europe, contact:
Hal Leonard Europe Limited
42 Wigmore Street
Marylebone, London, W1U 2RN
Email: info@halleonardeurope.com

In Australia, contact:
Hal Leonard Australia Pty. Ltd.
4 Lentara Court
Cheltenham, Victoria, 3192 Australia
Email: info@halleonard.com.au

Contents

ALL IS FOUND

Music and Lyrics by KRISTEN ANDERSON-LOPEZ
and ROBERT LOPEZ

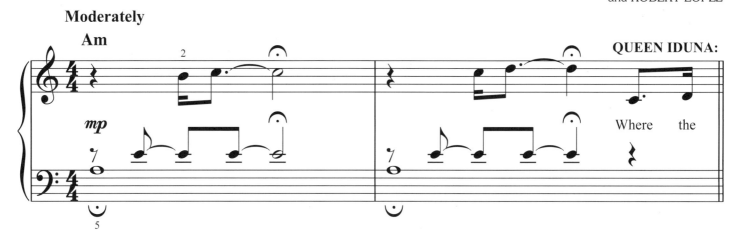

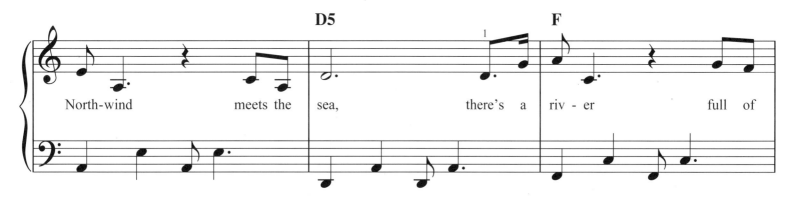

true lie the an - swers, and a path for you. Dive down

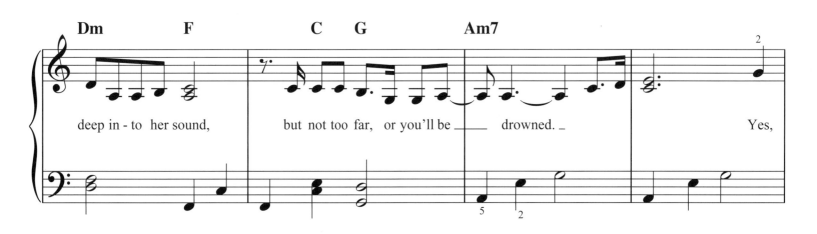

deep in - to her sound, but not too far, or you'll be drowned. Yes,

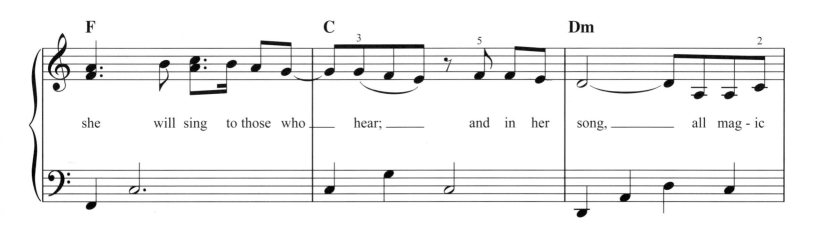

she will sing to those who hear; and in her song, all mag - ic

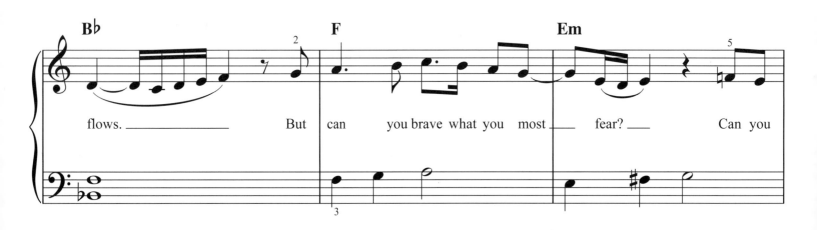

flows. But can you brave what you most fear? Can you

face   what the riv - er _____ knows? _____   Where the

North - wind _____ meets the _____ sea,   there's a   moth - er _____ full of _____

_____ mem-o - ry.   Come, my   dar - ling, home-ward bound: when all is

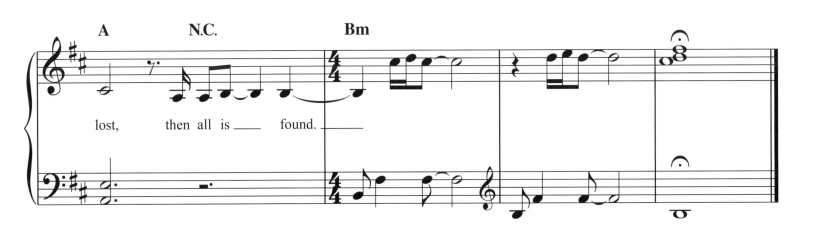

lost,   then all is _____ found. _____

SOME THINGS NEVER CHANGE

Music and Lyrics by KRISTEN ANDERSON-LOPEZ
and ROBERT LOPEZ

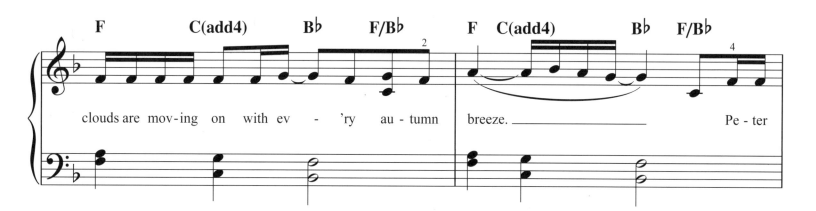

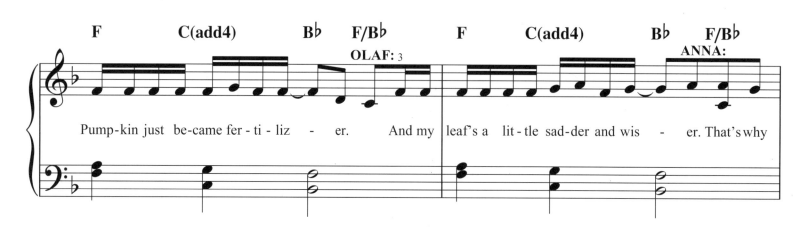

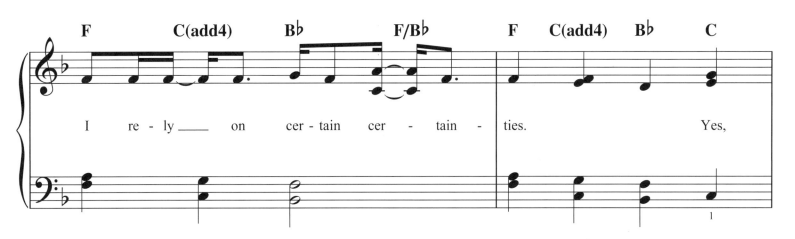

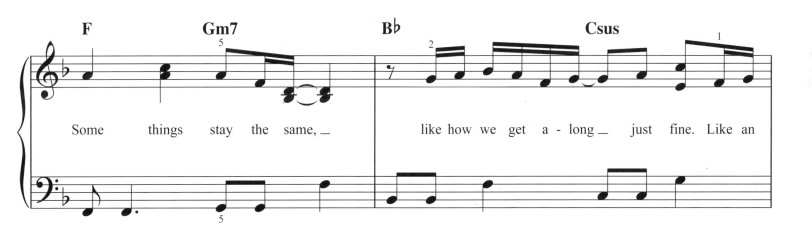

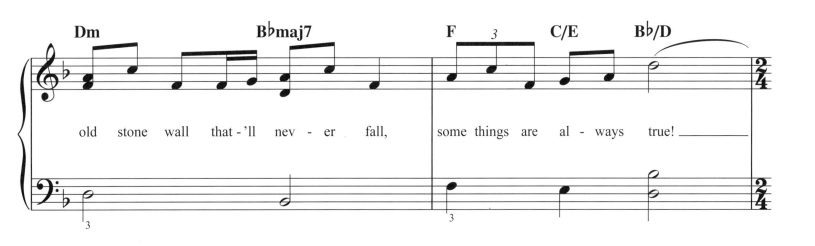

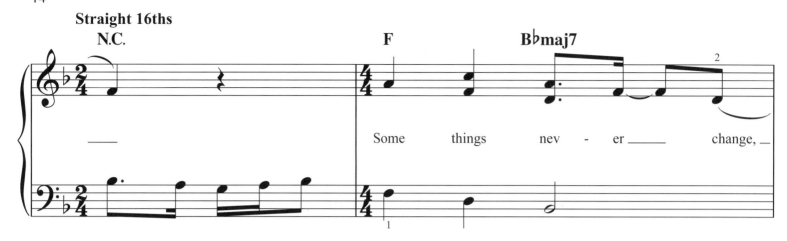

Straight 16ths

Some things nev - er _____ change, _____

like how I'm hold - ing on tight ___ to you.

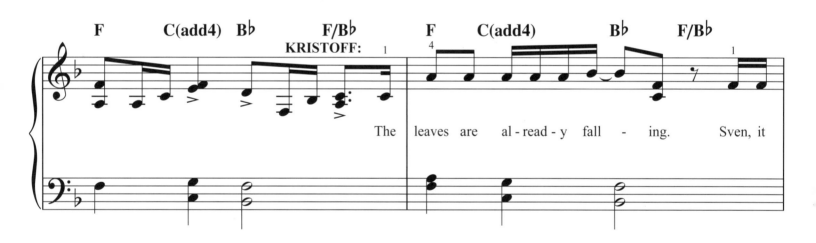

KRISTOFF:

The leaves are al - read - y fall - ing. Sven, it

feels like the fu - ture is call - ing! Are you

SVEN:

tell - ing me to - night you're gon - na get down on one

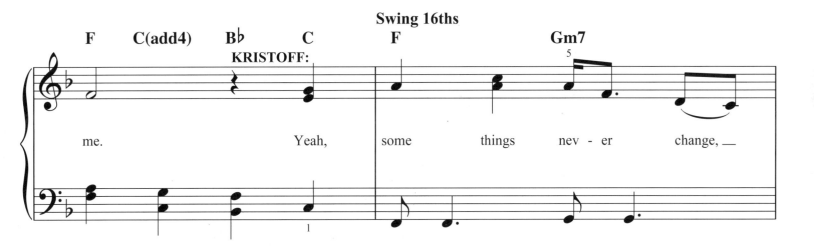

like how rein-deers are eas - i - er. But if I com-mit and I go for it, I'll

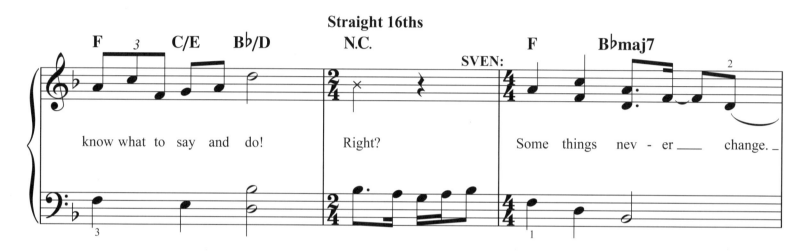

Straight 16ths

know what to say and do! Right? Some things nev - er___ change.___

KRISTOFF:

___ Sven, the pres-sure is all ___ on you.

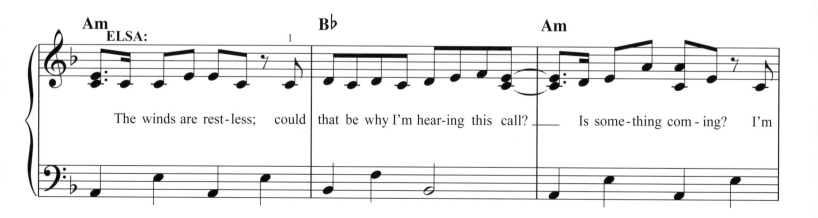

ELSA:

The winds are rest-less; could that be why I'm hear-ing this call? ___ Is some-thing com-ing? I'm

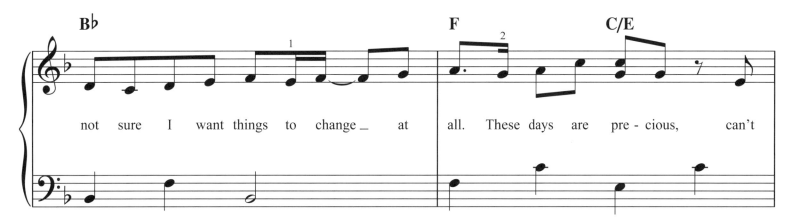

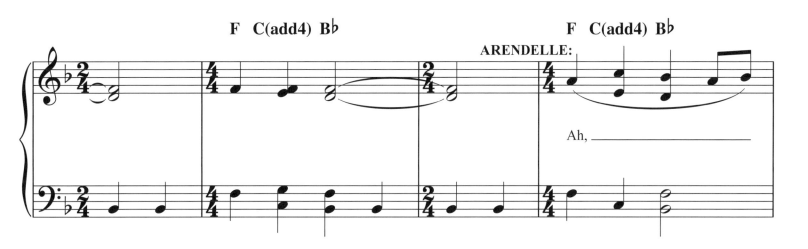

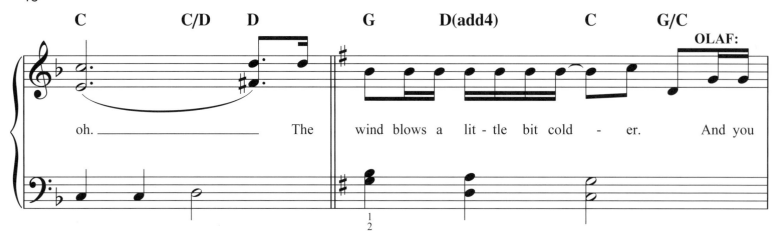

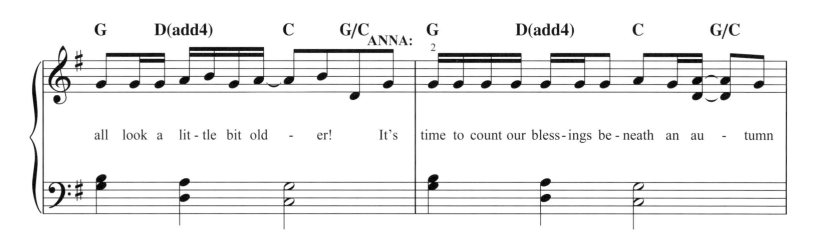

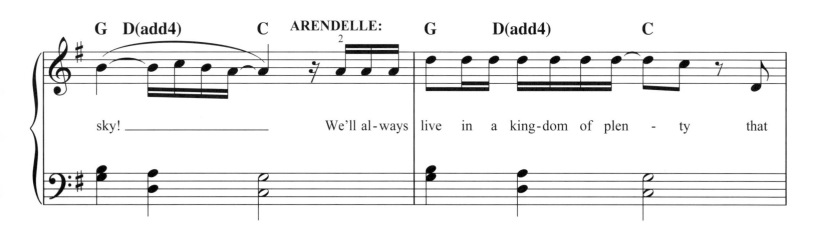

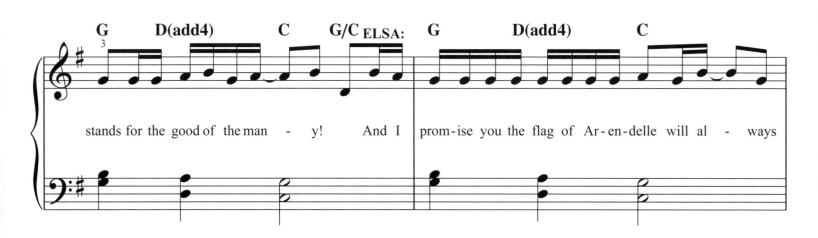

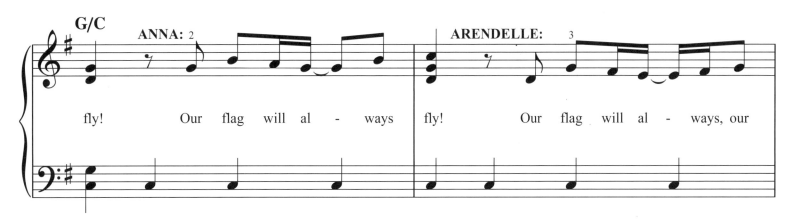

G/C **ANNA:** fly! Our flag will al - ways **ARENDELLE:** fly! Our flag will al - ways, our

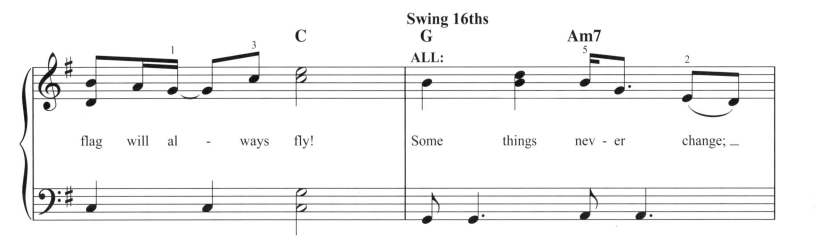

Swing 16ths
C **G** **Am7**
ALL:
flag will al - ways fly! Some things nev - er change; __

C **Dsus** **G** **Am7**
turn a - round, and the time __ has flown. Some things stay the same, _____

C **Dsus** **Em** **Cmaj7**
though the fu - ture re - mains __ un - known. May our good luck last, may our past be past.

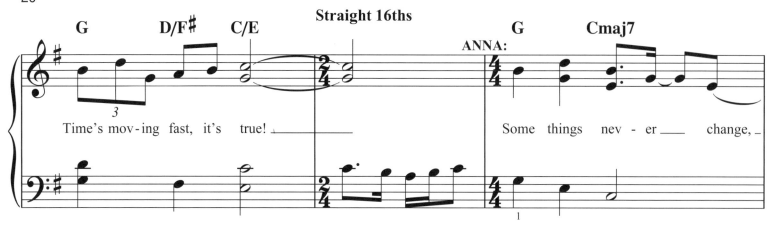

REINDEER(S) ARE BETTER THAN PEOPLE (CONT.)

Music and Lyrics by KRISTEN ANDERSON-LOPEZ
and ROBERT LOPEZ

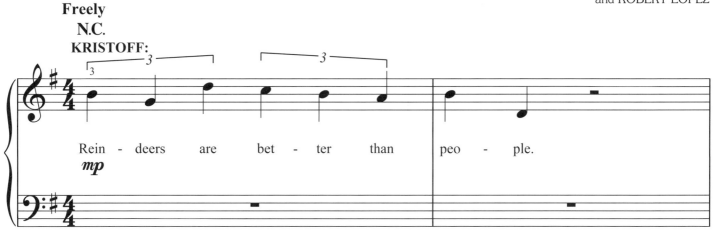

Freely
N.C.
KRISTOFF:

Rein - deers are bet - ter than peo - ple.

mp

Sven, why is love so hard? *(Spoken:)* You feel what you feel, and those

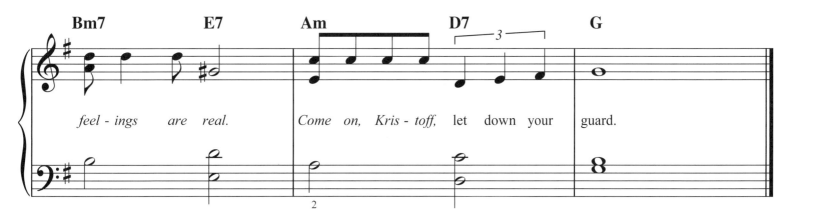

feel - ings are real. Come on, Kris - toff, let down your guard.

INTO THE UNKNOWN

Music and Lyrics by KRISTEN ANDERSON-LOPEZ
and ROBERT LOPEZ

Mysteriously

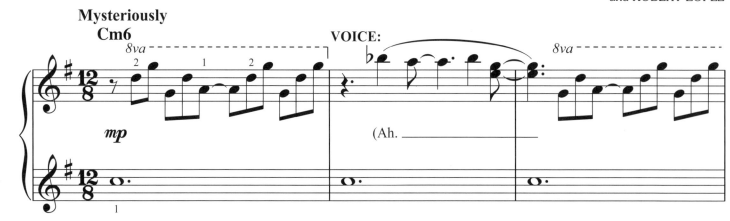

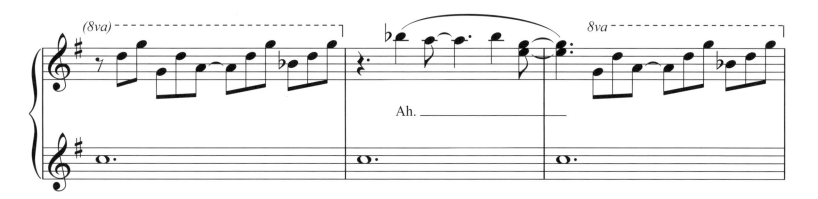

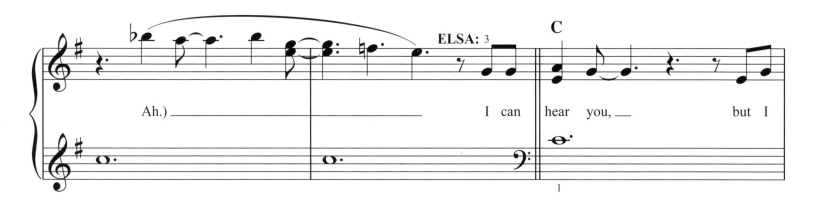

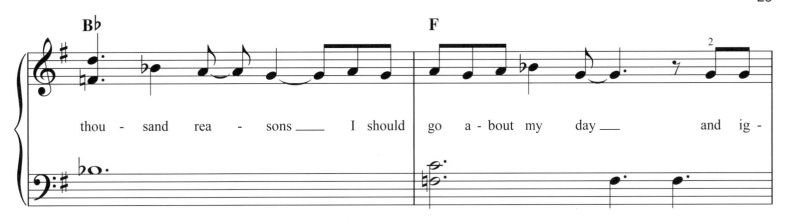

thou - sand rea - sons ___ I should go a - bout my day ___ and ig-

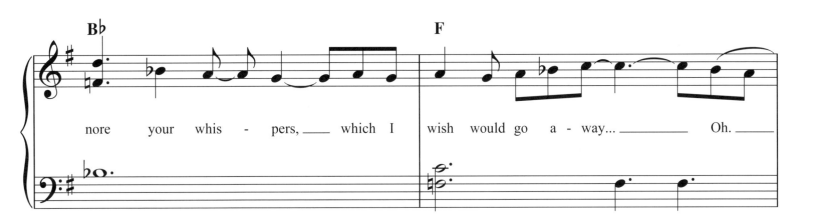

nore your whis - pers, ___ which I wish would go a - way... _____ Oh. ___

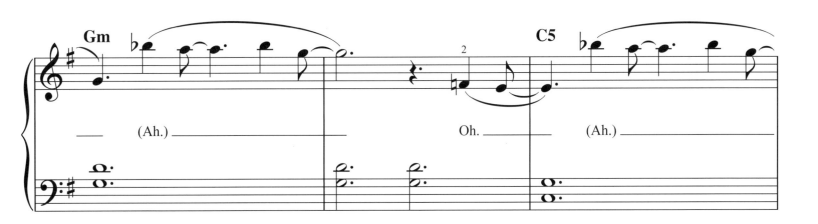

___ (Ah.) _____ Oh. (Ah.)

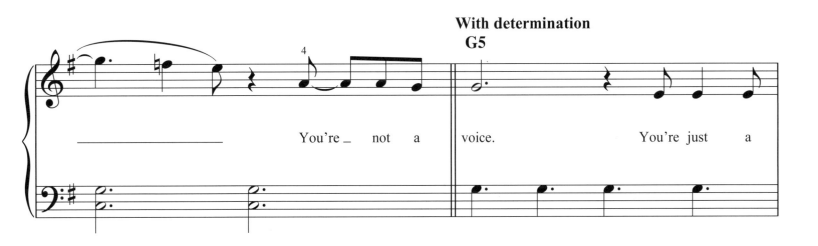

_____ You're _ not a voice. You're just a

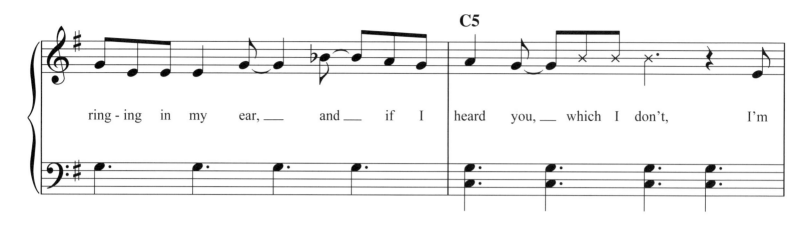

ring - ing in my ear, ___ and ___ if I heard you, ___ which I don't, I'm

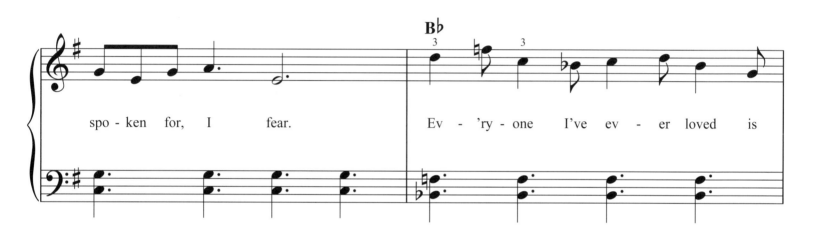

spo - ken for, I fear. Ev - 'ry - one I've ev - er loved is

here with - in these walls. ___ I'm sor - ry, se - cret si - ren, but I'm

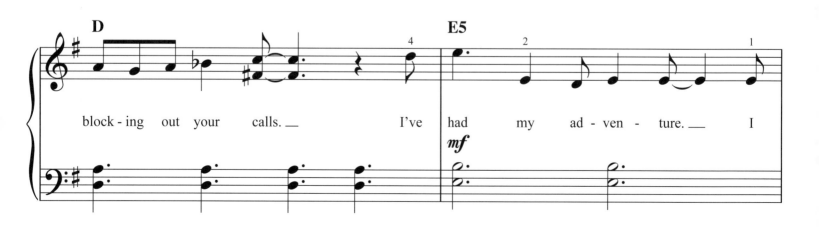

block - ing out your calls. ___ I've had my ad - ven - ture. ___ I

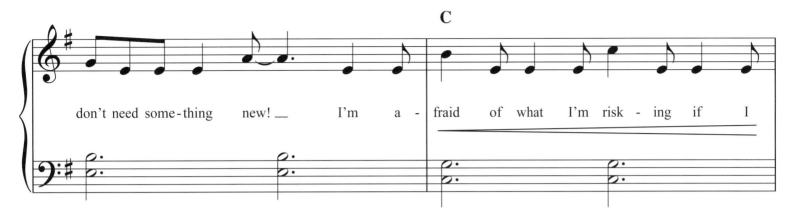

don't need some-thing new! __ I'm a - fraid of what I'm risk - ing if I

fol - low you in - to the un - known... in - to the un - known... _

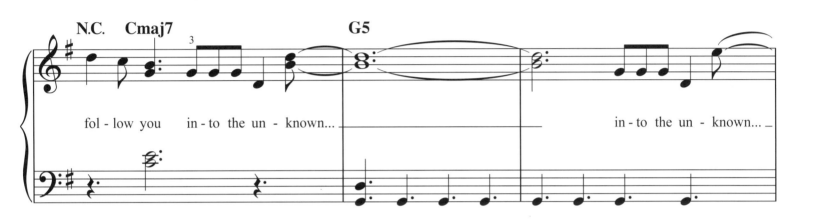

in - to the un - known!

(Ah. ___ Ah.) ___

Gm6

What — do you want? 'Cause you've been keep-ing me a - wake. — Are you

C7   **N.C.**

here — to dis-tract me — so I make a big mis - take? — Or are you

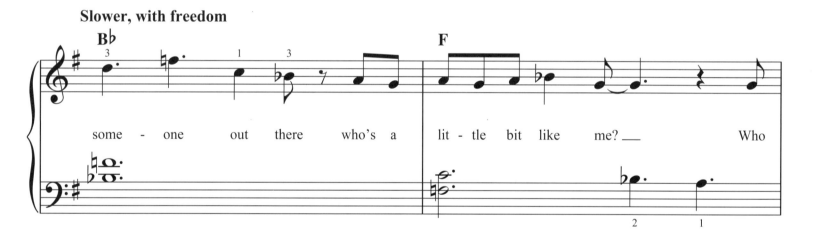

Slower, with freedom

B♭   **F**

some - one out there who's a lit - tle bit like me? — Who

C   **Dsus**   **N.C.**

knows deep down I'm not where I'm meant to be? — Ev - 'ry
rit.

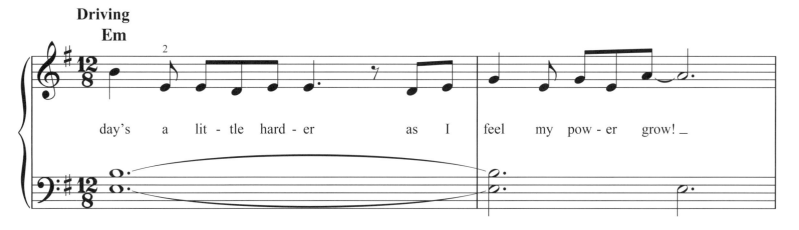

Driving

day's a lit - tle hard - er as I feel my pow - er grow! _

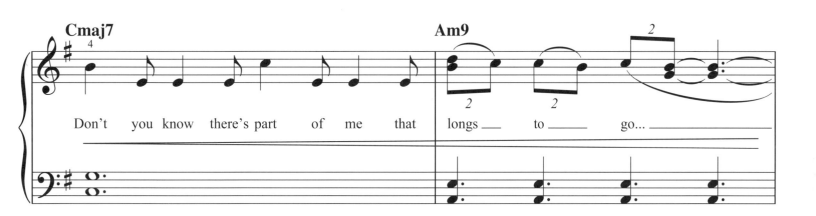

Don't you know there's part of me that longs __ to __ go... _

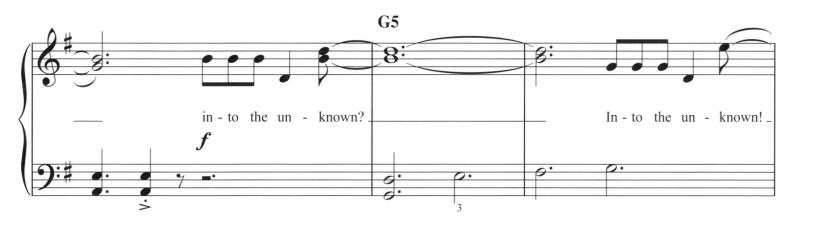

in - to the un - known? _ In - to the un - known! _

In - to the un - known!

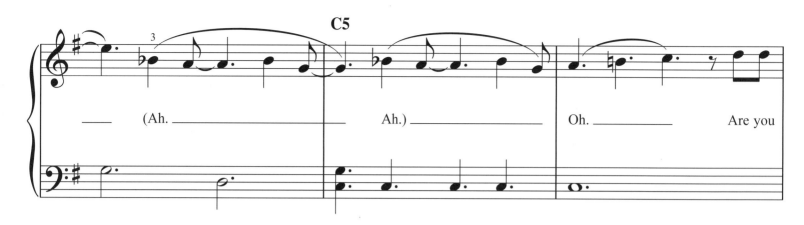

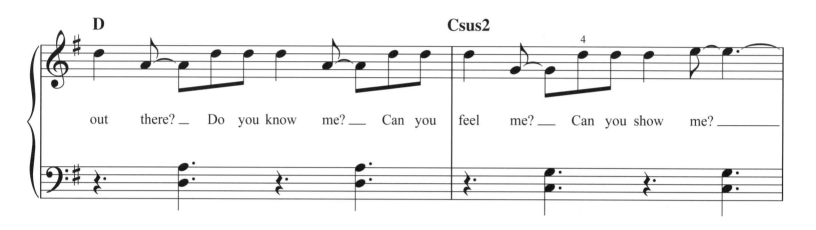

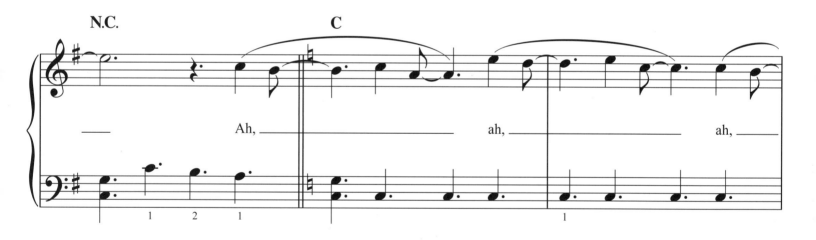

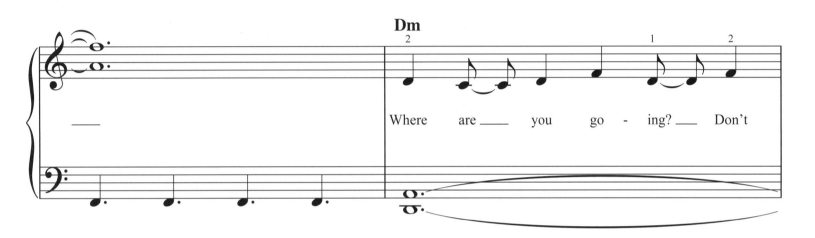

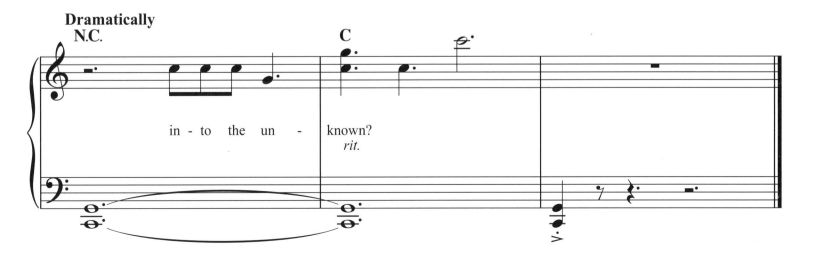

WHEN I AM OLDER

Music and Lyrics by KRISTEN ANDERSON-LOPEZ
and ROBERT LOPEZ

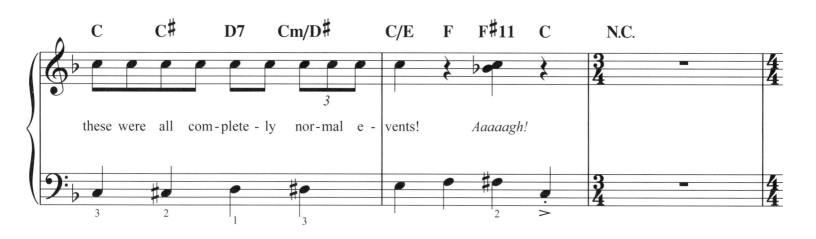

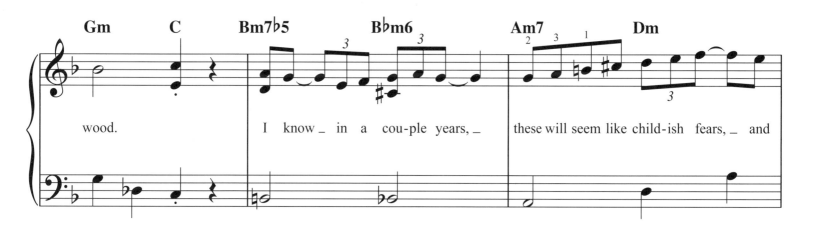

so I know, this is - n't bad, it's good! *(Spoken:) Excuse me.*

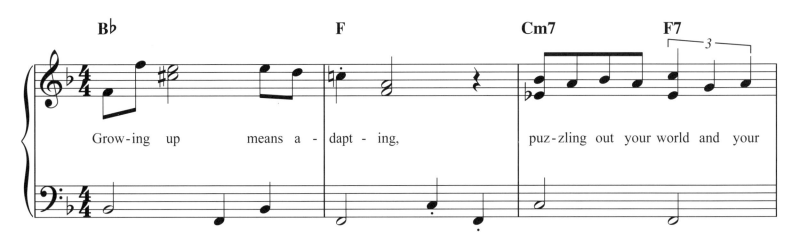

Grow - ing up means a - dapt - ing, puz - zling out your world and your

place! When I'm more ma - ture, I'll feel to - tal - ly se - cure be - ing

watched by some - thing__ with a creep - y, creep - y face.__ AAAAH!!!, AAAAH!!!

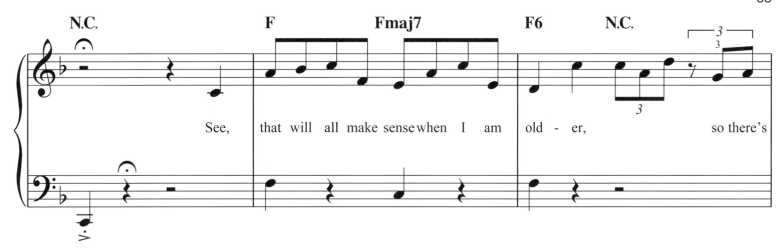

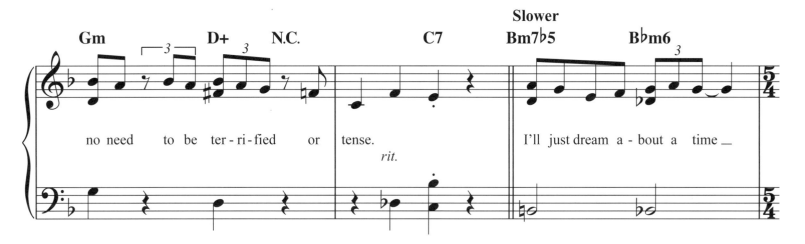

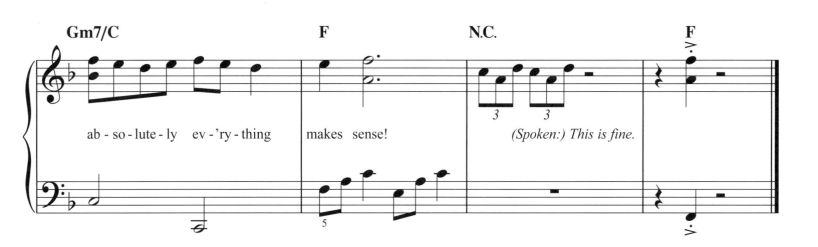

LOST IN THE WOODS

Music and Lyrics by KRISTEN ANDERSON-LOPEZ
and ROBERT LOPEZ

Moderately, in 2

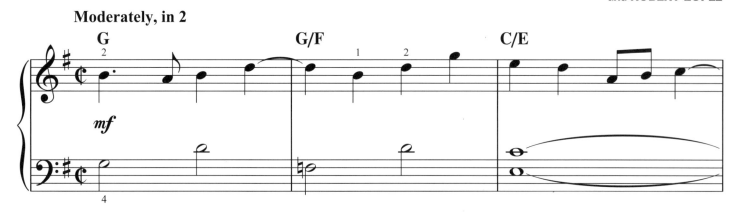

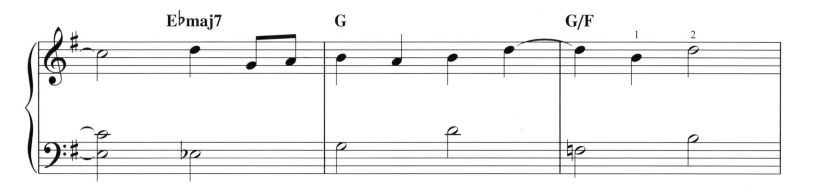

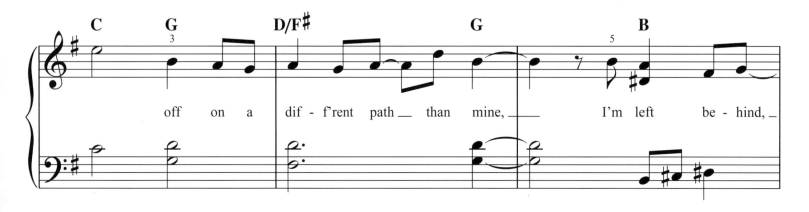

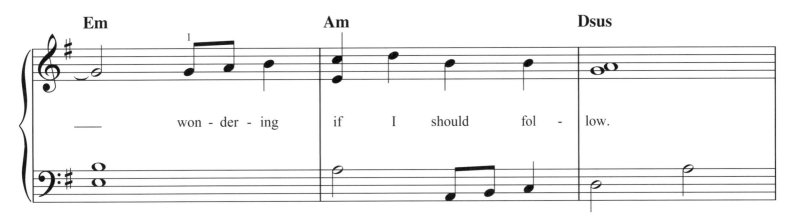

this what it feels _____ like to be grow - ing a - part? _____

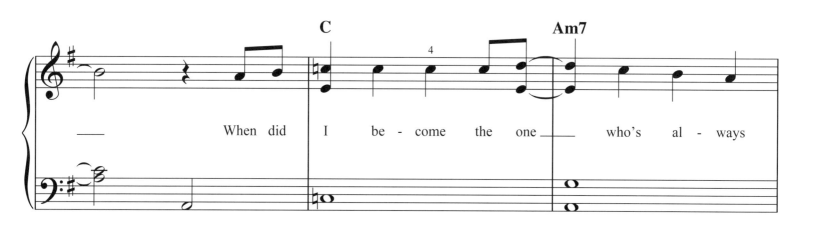

_____ When did I be - come the one _____ who's al - ways

chas - ing your heart? _____ Now I turn a - round _____ and find _____

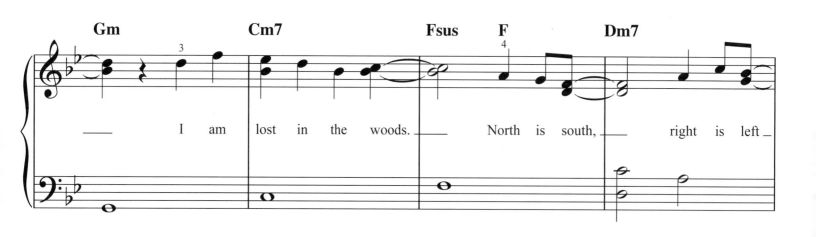

_____ I am lost in the woods. _____ North is south, _____ right is left _____

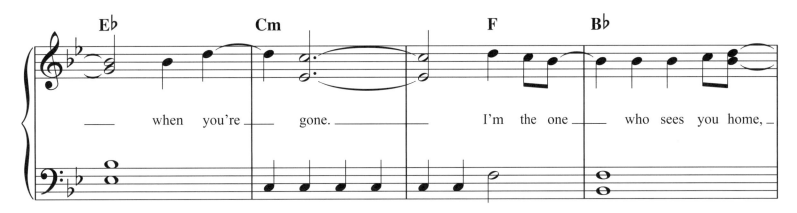

when you're _____ gone. _____ I'm the one ____ who sees you home, _

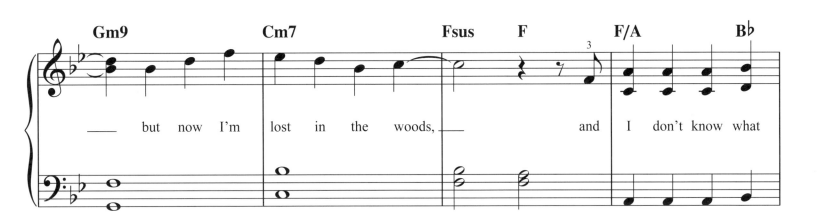

_____ but now I'm lost in the woods, _____ and I don't know what

path you are on. _____ I'm lost in the woods. _

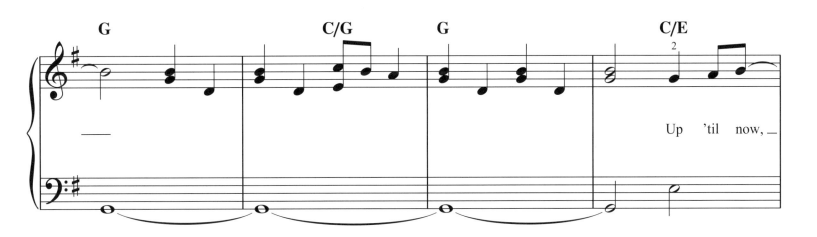

Up 'til now, _

the next step was a ques - tion of how; ____

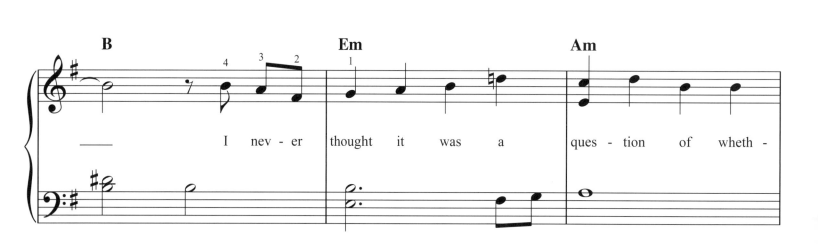

____ I nev - er thought it was a ques - tion of wheth -

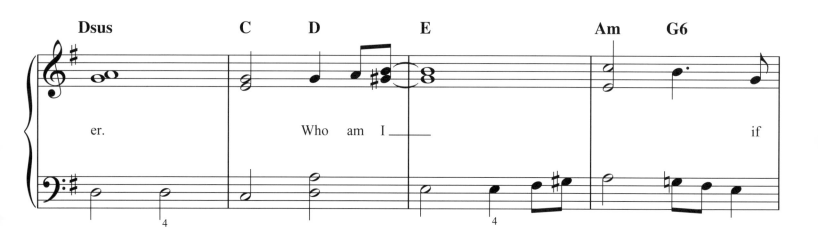

er. Who am I _____ if

I'm not your guy? _____ Where am I if

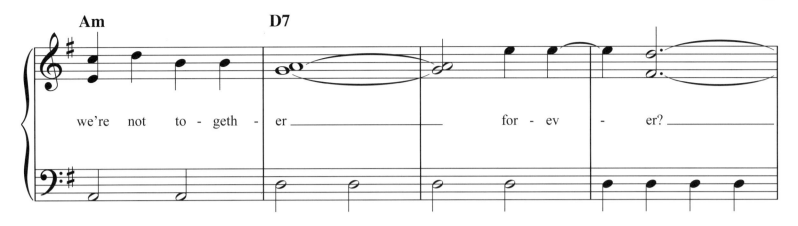

we're not to - geth - er _____ for - ev - er? _____

_____ Now I know you're my true North, _____ 'cause I am

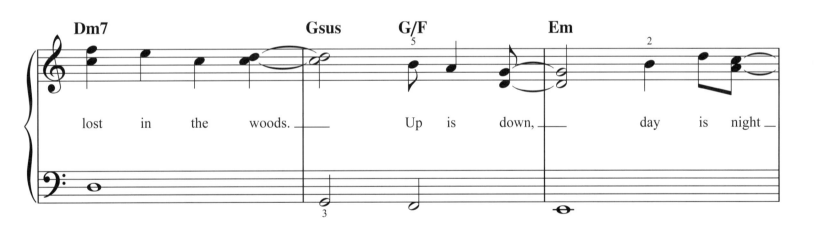

lost in the woods. _____ Up is down, _____ day is night

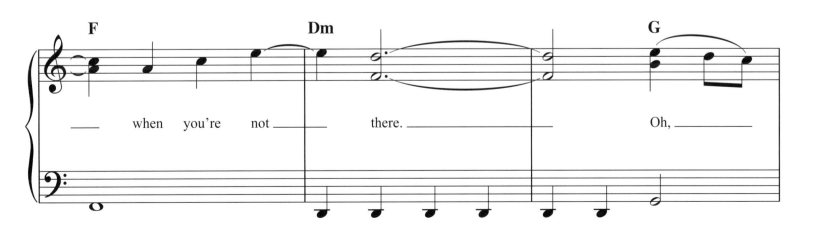

_____ when you're not _____ there. _____ Oh, _____

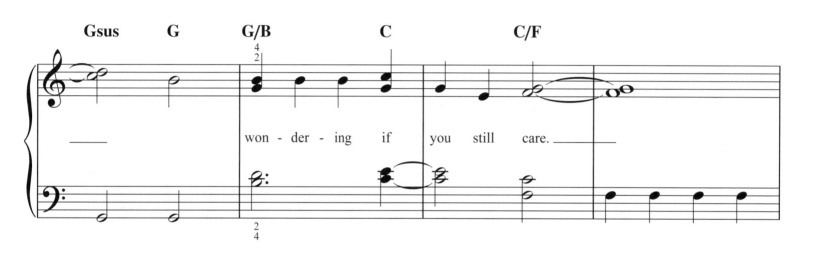

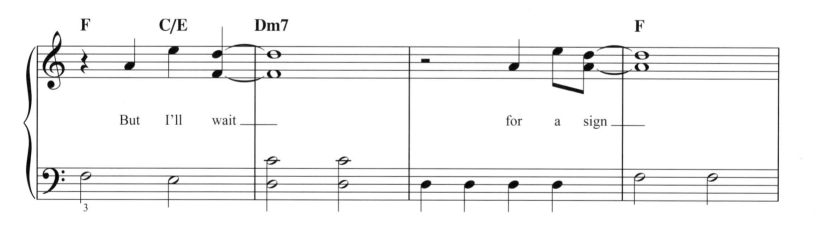

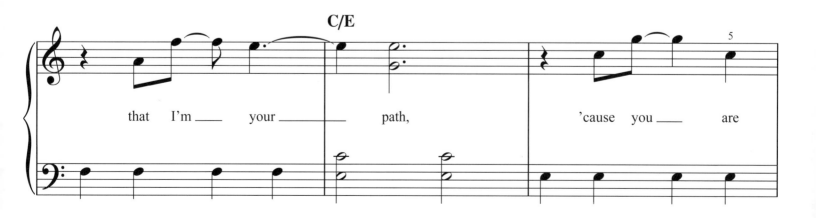

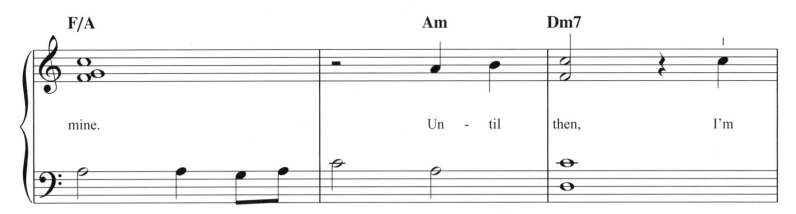

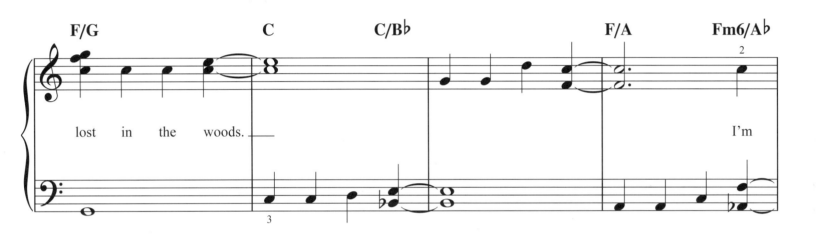

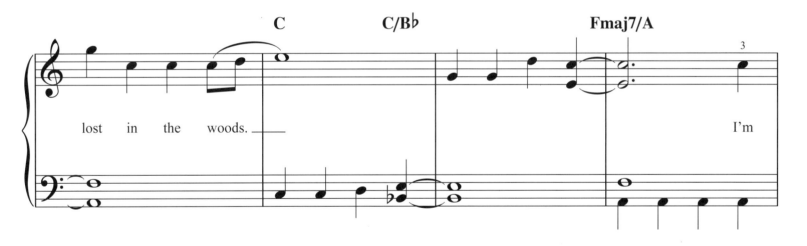

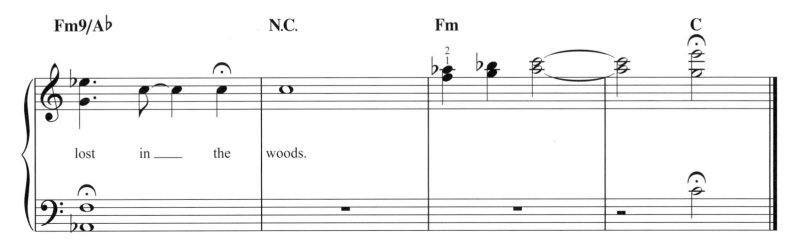

THE NEXT RIGHT THING

Music and Lyrics by KRISTEN ANDERSON-LOPEZ
and ROBERT LOPEZ

Moderately slow, with freedom

ANNA: I've seen dark be-fore, but not like

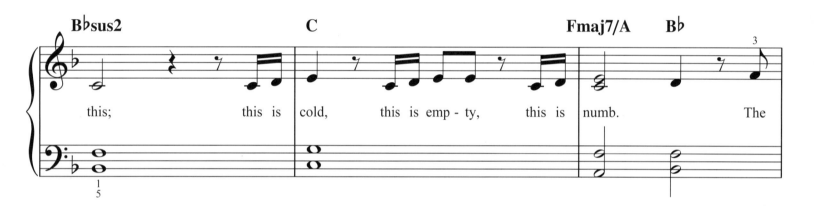

this; this is cold, this is emp-ty, this is numb. The

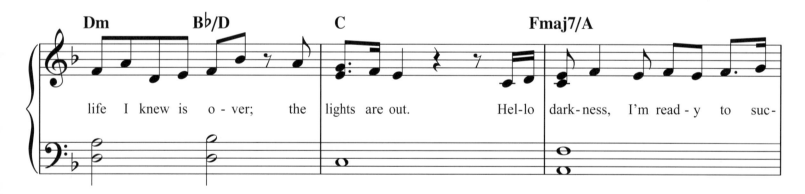

life I knew is o-ver; the lights are out. Hel-lo dark-ness, I'm read-y to suc-

cumb. I fol-low you a-round, _ I al-ways have, but you've

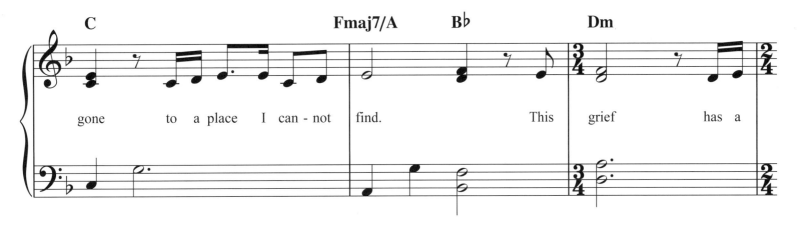

gone   to a place I can-not find.   This   grief   has a

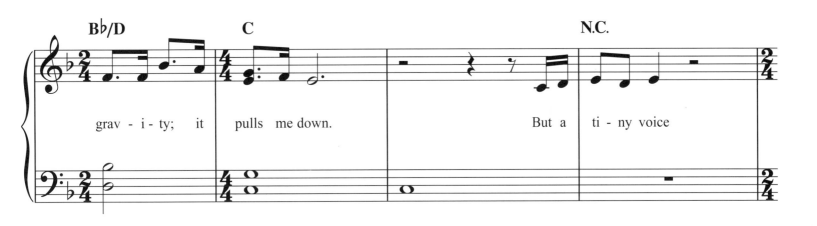

grav - i - ty;   it pulls me down.   But a ti - ny voice

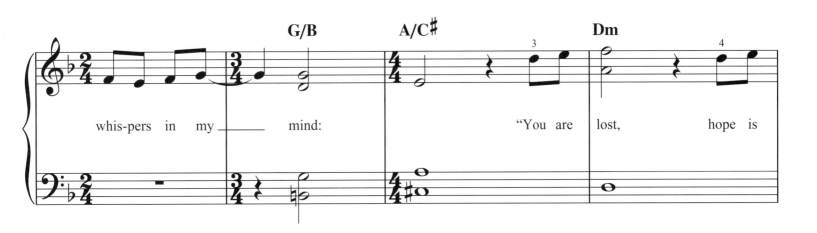

whis-pers in my ____ mind: "You are lost,   hope is

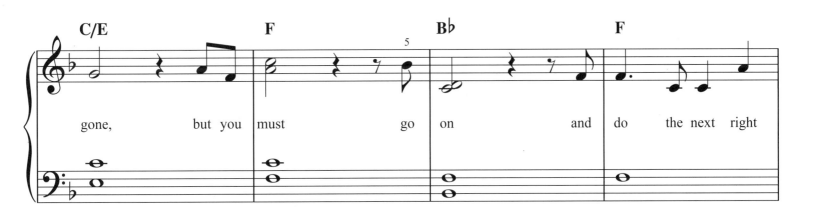

gone,   but you must   go on   and do the next right

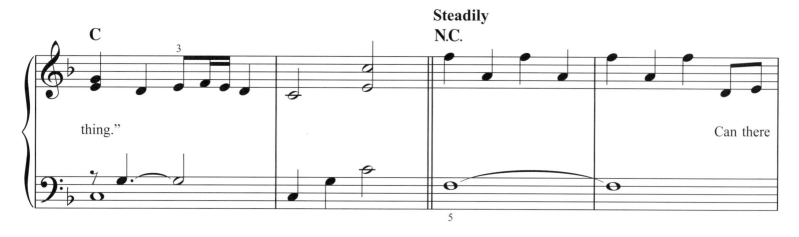

Steadily

C

N.C.

thing."   Can there

Dm/F   **B♭sus2**   **C**

be   a day   be-yond this   night?   I   don't know an-y-more what is

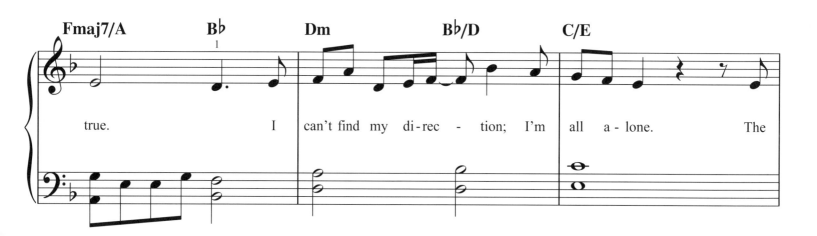

Fmaj7/A   **B♭**   **Dm**   **B♭/D**   **C/E**

true.   I   can't find my di-rec - tion; I'm   all a-lone.   The

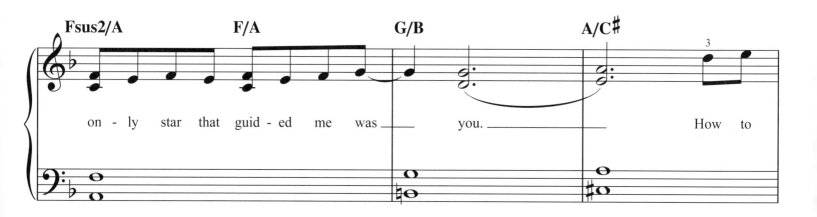

Fsus2/A   **F/A**   **G/B**   **A/C♯**

on-ly star that guid-ed me was____ you.____   How to

rise from the floor when it's not you _____ I'm ris - ing

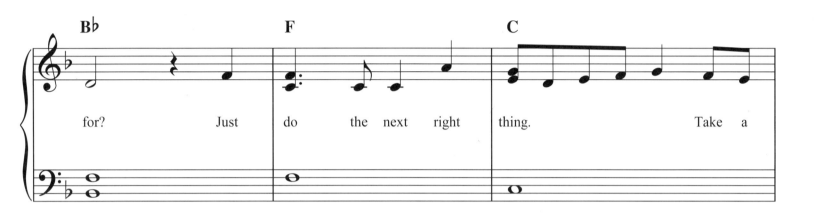

for? Just do the next right thing. Take a

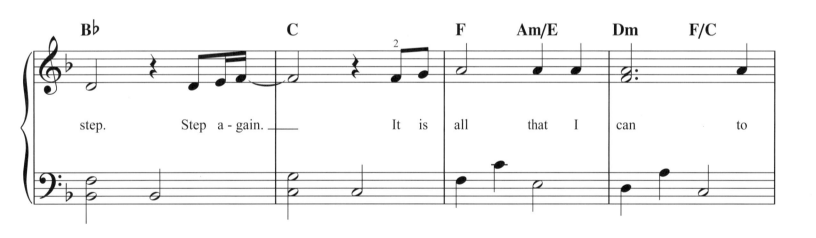

step. Step a - gain. ___ It is all that I can to

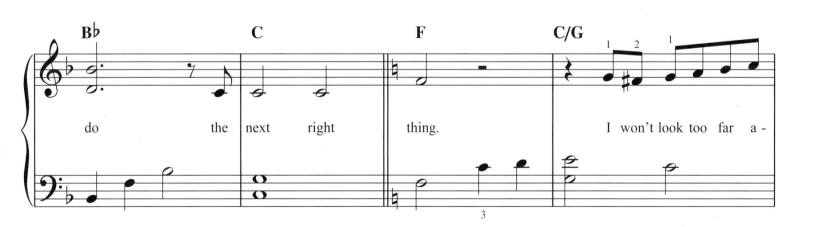

do the next right thing. I won't look too far a -

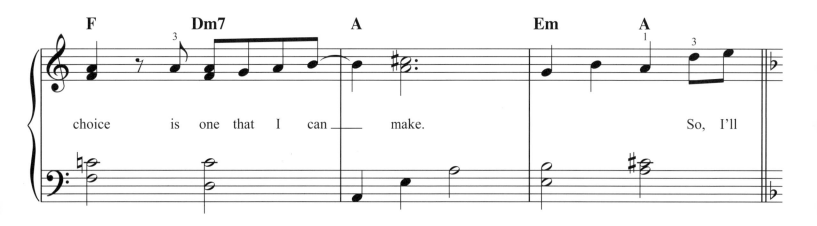

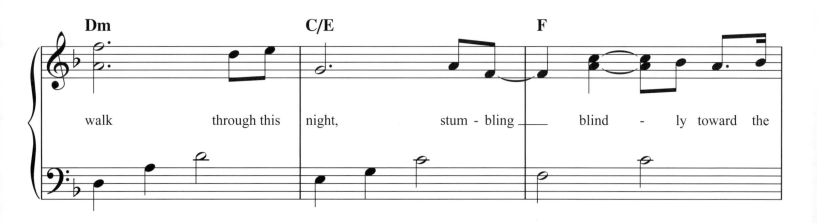

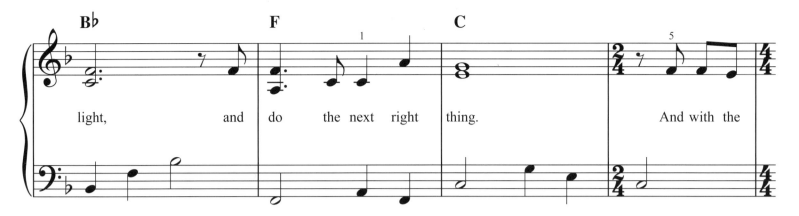

light, and do the next right thing. And with the

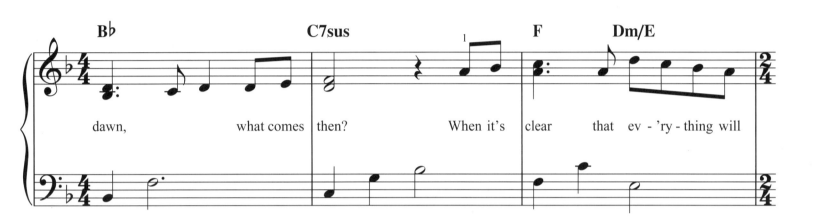

dawn, what comes then? When it's clear that ev-'ry-thing will

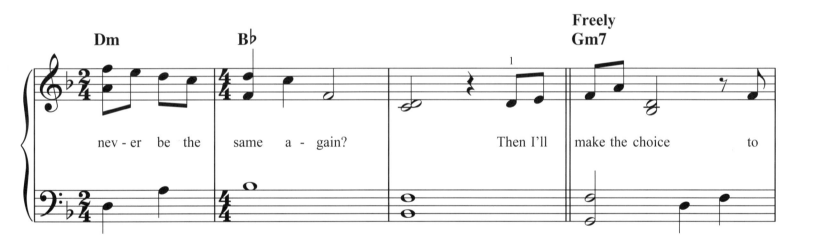

nev-er be the same a-gain? Then I'll make the choice to

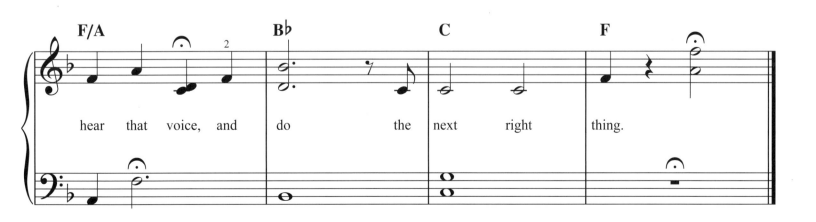

hear that voice, and do the next right thing.

SHOW YOURSELF

Music and Lyrics by KRISTEN ANDERSON-LOPEZ
and ROBERT LOPEZ

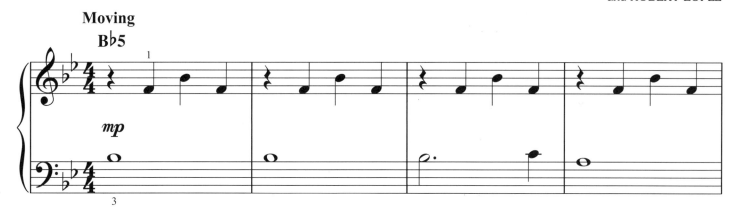

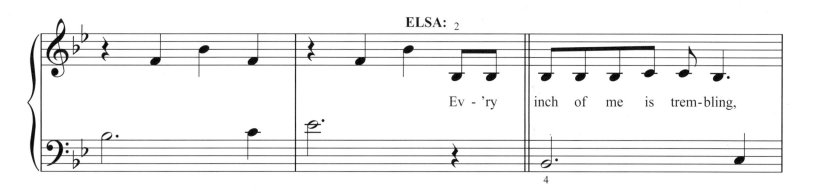

sense   you   there, __   like   a   friend I've   al - ways   known. ____

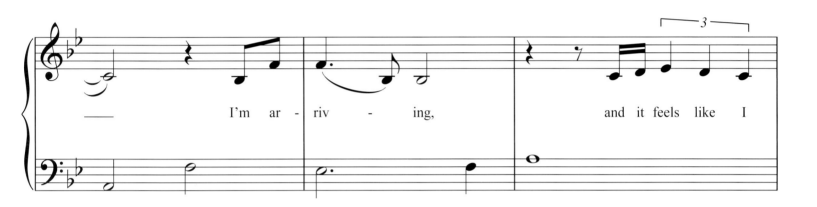

____   I'm   ar - riv - ing,   and it feels like   I

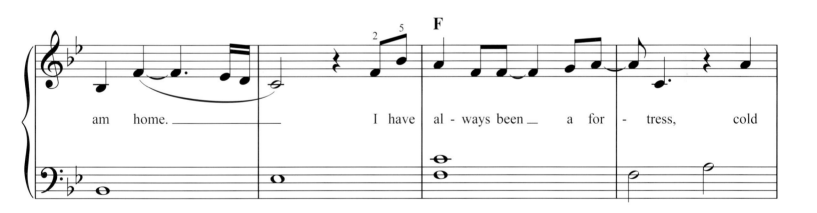

am   home. ____   I have   al - ways been __   a for - tress,   cold

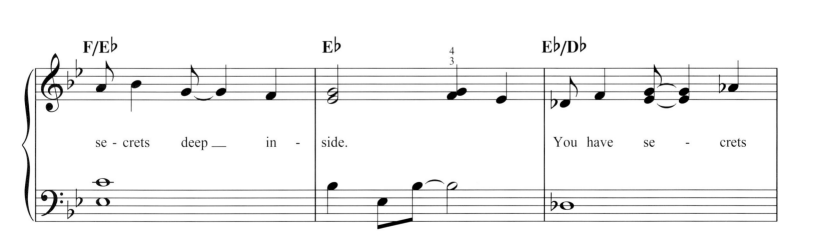

se - crets   deep __   in - side.   You have   se - crets

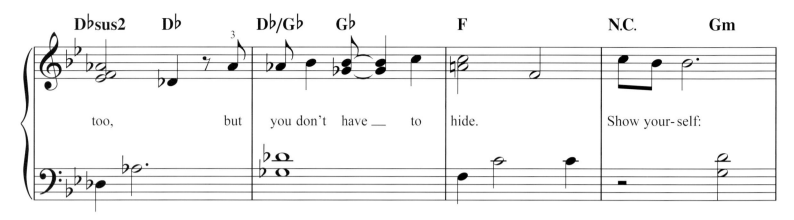

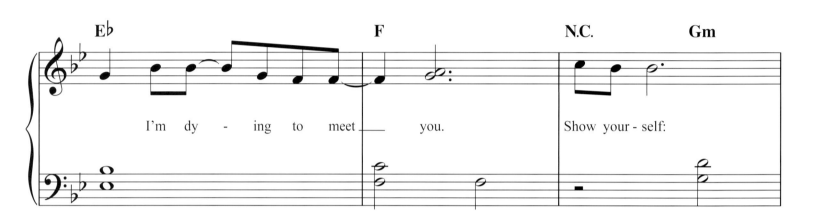

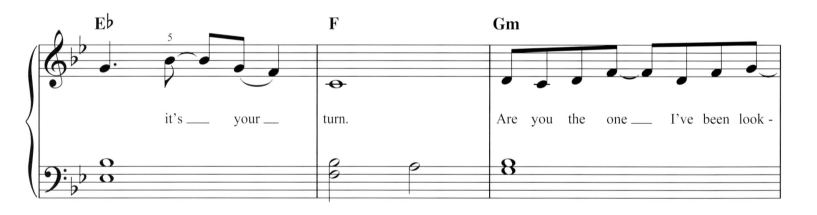

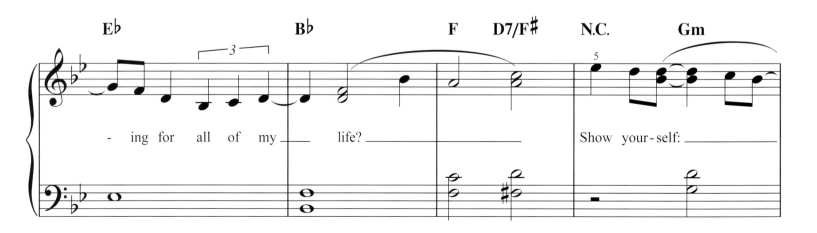

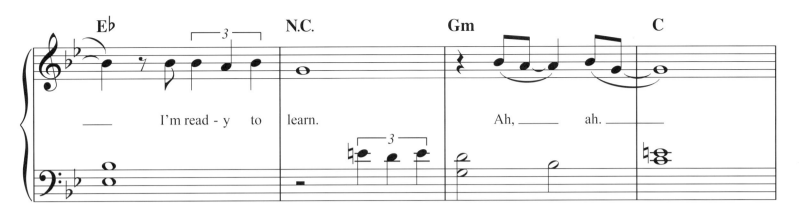

I'm read-y to learn.   Ah, _____ ah. _____

Ah, _____ ah. _____   I've nev-er felt so cer-tain.

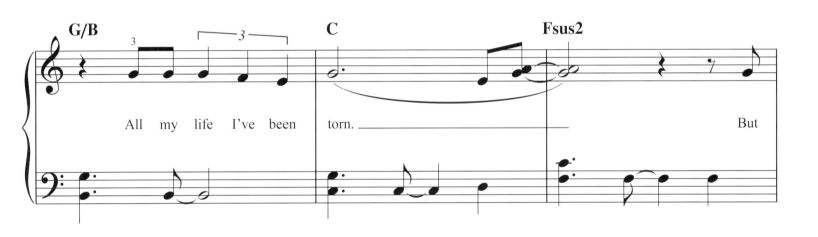

All my life I've been   torn. _____   But

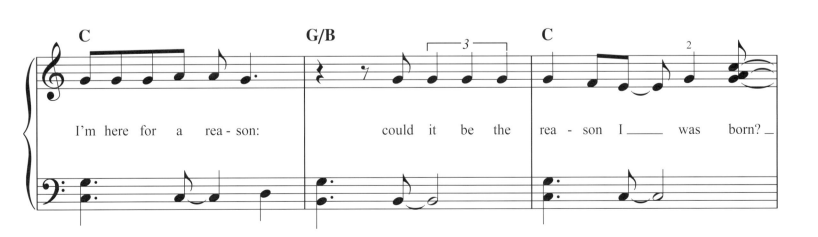

I'm here for a rea-son: could it be the   rea-son I _____ was born? _____

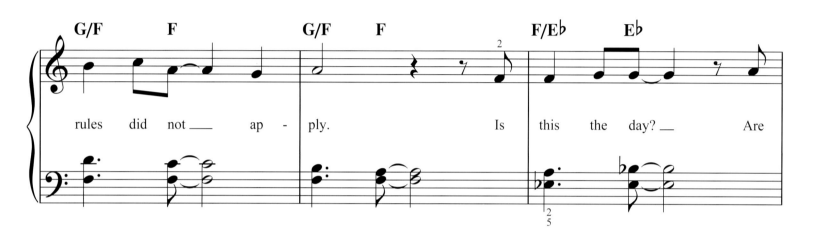

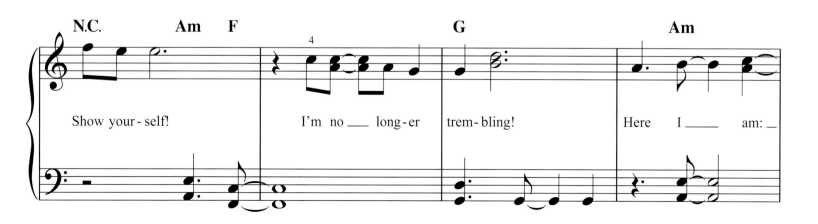

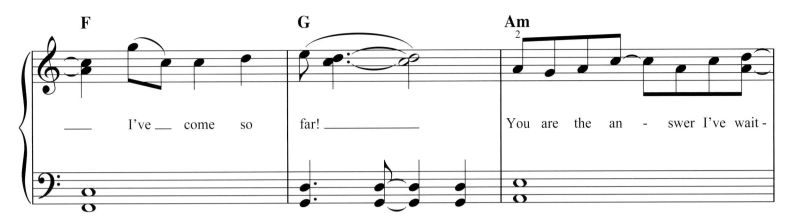

I've __ come so far! _____ You are the an - swer I've wait -

- ed for all of my __ life! _____ Oh, show your-self: ____

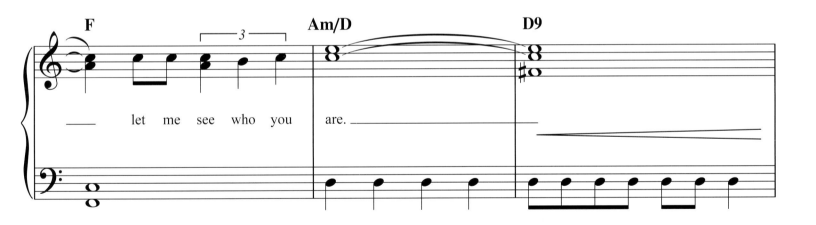

__ let me see who you are. _____

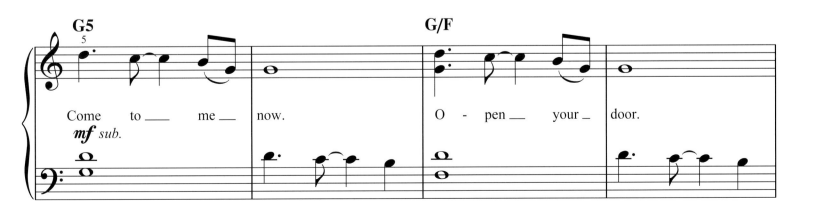

Come to __ me __ now. O - pen __ your __ door.

Am7sus

Don't make ___ me ___ wait

F

one mo - ment more!

cresc. poco a poco

C

Oh, ___

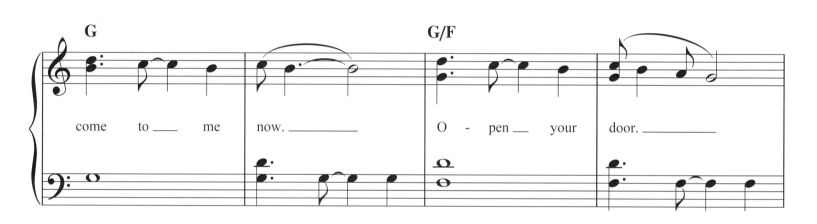

G

come to ___ me

now. _____

G/F

O - pen ___ your door. _____

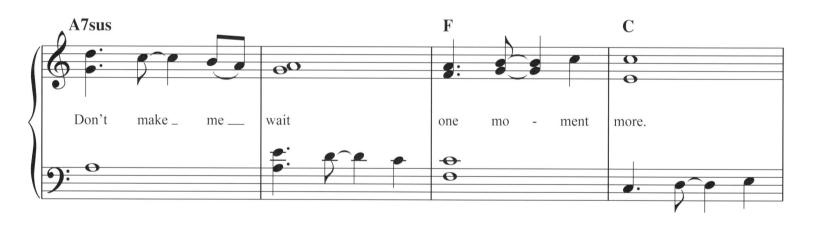

A7sus

Don't make ___ me ___ wait

F

one mo - ment more.

C

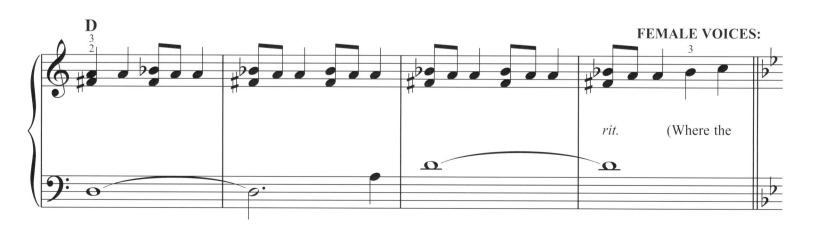

D

FEMALE VOICES:

rit. (Where the

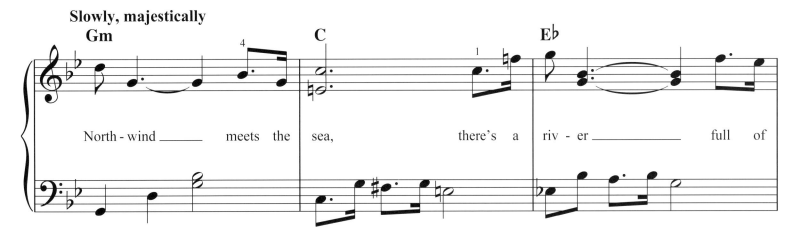

Slowly, majestically

North - wind _____ meets the sea, there's a riv - er _____ full of

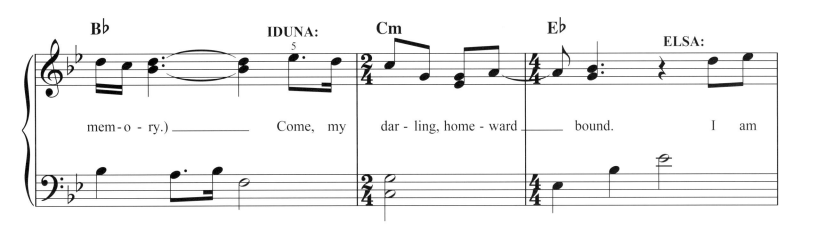

mem - o - ry.) _____ Come, my dar - ling, home - ward _____ bound. I am

Moving, as before

found! Show your - self! _ Step in - to your pow -

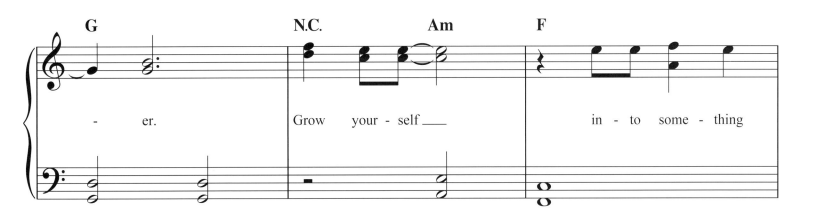

- er. Grow your - self ___ in - to some - thing

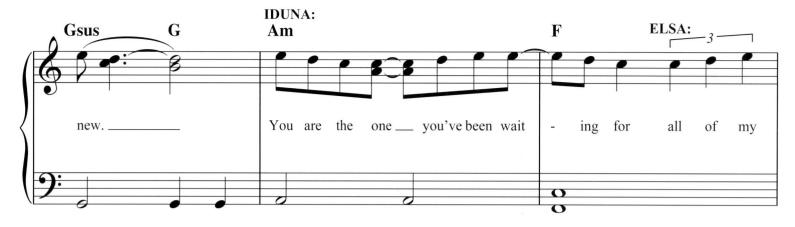

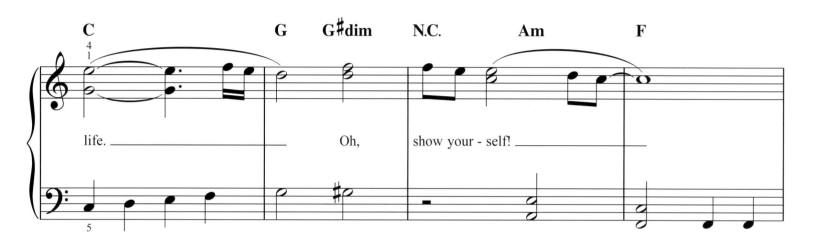

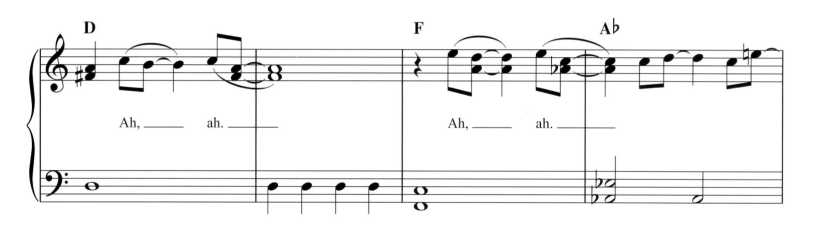

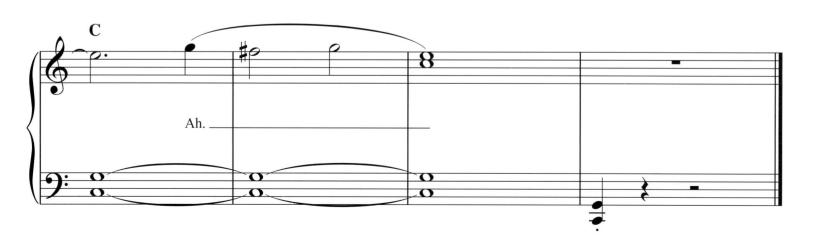